UNCOVERING HISTORY
THE CELTS

Copyright © 2003 McRae Books Srl, Florence (Italy)

Everyday Life of the Celts
was created and produced by McRae Books
Borgo Santa Croce, 8 – Florence (Italy)
e-mail: info@mcraebooks.com

SERIES EDITOR Anne McRae
TEXT Neil Grant
ILLUSTRATIONS Manuela Cappon, Luisa Della Porta, Paola
Ravaglia, Andrea Ricciardi di Gaudesi, Studio Inklink,
Studio Stalio (Alessandro
Cantucci, Fabiano Fabbrucci,
Andrea Morandi)
GRAPHIC DESIGN Marco
Nardi
LAYOUT Piero Bongiorno
EDITING Anne McRae
REPRO Litocolor, Florence
PICTURE RESEARCH Elzbieta
Gontarska

Published in the United States
by Smart Apple Media
1980 Lookout Drive, North
Mankato, Minnesota 56003

Printed and bound in Italy

Library of Congress Cataloging-in-Publication Data
Grant, Neil.
Everyday life of the Celts / by Neil Grant ; illustrated by Manuela
Cappon.
p. cm. — (Uncovering history)
Includes index.
Contents: Origins — The Celtic world — Religion — The Druids —
Burial — Farming and food — The Celts at war — Daily life — Celtic
homesteads — Technology — Art — Festivals — Villages and towns —
Fun and games — Celts and Romans — Romanized Celts — Trade —
The Celtic fringe — The Celtic revival.
ISBN 1-58340-252-7
1. Celts—Juvenile literature 2. Civilization, Celtic—Juvenile literature. 3.
Celts—Social life and customs—Juvenile literature.
[1. Celts. 2. Civilization, Celtic.] I. Cappon, Manuela, ill. II.
Title. III. Series.

D70.G73 2003
930'.04916—dc21   2003042351

First Edition
9 8 7 6 5 4 3 2 1

Neil Grant

EVERYDAY LIFE OF THE

CELTS

Illustrations by Manuela Cappon, Studio Stalio

Smart Apple Media

Table of Contents

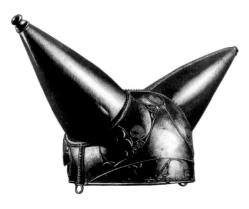

Origins   8

The Celtic World   10

Religion   12

The Druids   14

Burial   16

Farming and Food   18

The Celts at War   20

Society and Daily Life   22

Celtic Homesteads   24

Technology   26

Art   28

Festivals   30

Villages and Towns   32

Fun and Games   34

Celts and Romans   36

Romanized Celts   38

Trade and Travel   40

The Celtic Fringes   42

The Celts Live On   44

Index   46

Introduction

The Celts lived in a large part of Europe between about 500 B.C. and A.D. 500. The lands of the Celts at their largest stretched from northern Scotland to southern Portugal and across the whole of Europe. The Celts even crossed into Asia, settling in Galatia, in Anatolia (modern Turkey). The Celts were not a single people. In every country where they lived, they were divided into many tribes that often fought each other. The Celts of Britain and Ireland differed from their neighbors in Gaul (a larger version of modern France), and both were different again from the Celts of Iberia (modern Spain and Portugal). They spoke several languages, but the languages were closely related, like the surviving Celtic languages of Breton and Welsh are today. The people of all the Celtic lands shared many of the same ideas, the same customs, and the same way of living—the same "culture." Because the Celts themselves did not keep written records, learning about them depends upon the accounts written by people from the more advanced ancient societies of Greece and Rome (which eventually conquered most of the Celtic world). Equally important are the discoveries of archaeologists: it is surprising how much archaeologists can learn from the contents of an ancient grave. Finally, scholars can study the writings of later Celts, especially Irish monks who, from about A.D. 700, wrote down Celtic folk tales that had been told and retold for many centuries.

BEGINNING OF THE HALLSTATT CULTURE *c. 1200 B.C.*

BEGINNING OF THE IRON AGE *c. 750 B.C.*

CELTS SETTLE IN IBERIA *c. 600 B.C.*

CELTS TRADE WITH GREEK MERCHANTS AT MASSALIA (MARSEILLE) *c. 500 B.C.*
FIRST MENTION OF THE CELTS IN WRITING (GREEK) *c. 550 B.C.*

THE GAULS ATTACK ROME *387 B.C.*

CELTS INVADE GREECE *c. 280 B.C.* AND SETTLE IN GALATIA, ASIA MINOR

OPPIDA (TOWNS) BUILT IN CELTIC KINGDOMS *c. 200 B.C.*

CAESAR CONQUERS GAUL *58–52 B.C.*

ROMANS DEFEAT THE CELTS IN EASTERN EUROPE, IBERIA *c. 20 B.C.*

ROMANS INVADE CELTIC BRITAIN *A.D. 43*

GERMANIC TRIBES SETTLE IN GAUL AND INVADE BRITAIN *c. 350*

CHRISTIANITY REACHES IRELAND *c. 400*

Mining

The wealth of the Hallstatt chiefdoms came partly from mining iron ore, copper, and other minerals, which were in great demand in the Mediterranean world. This picture (right) shows a Hallstatt salt mine. Although the Celts were not especially good at big engineering projects, this mine used efficient technology (and saved workers from the job of working underground). A stream was made to run through the mine. It washed out the rock salt, then flowed, via wooden channels, into salt pans, where the sun dried up the water, leaving the salt.

Origins

Hallstatt is a small, pretty Austrian town backed by mountains, on which prehistoric salt mines can still be seen. Salt, once as valuable as gold, is a preservative, and at Hallstatt, archaeologists have found rich remains of a way of life now called the Hallstatt culture. Beginning around 1200 B.C. in central Europe, the Hallstatt culture eventually spread to Britain, Spain, and the Balkans. It lasted until the fifth century B.C., when it was overtaken by the La Tène culture (also named after a famous archaeological site, in Switzerland). The Hallstatt people were Celts. They lived in small chiefdoms made up of farms, villages, and hill-forts. Their culture changed much over the centuries. The biggest change was from bronze- to iron-working in the eighth century B.C., which brought greater wealth and an increase in population.

The Celts did not use buttons. They fastened their cloaks with pins that worked like modern safety pins, with many variations dictated by fashion. The chains and triangles attached to this sixth-century bronze pin are just decoration.

Technology and art

The Hallstatt Celts were expert craftsmen, in many ways the equals of their Roman conquerors. Some of the mining and metalwork techniques of the Hallstatt culture were not surpassed in Europe until the 18th century. A late-Hallstatt cart, for example, was basically no different from the farm carts used 2,000 years later. Instinctive artists, the Celts decorated everything with their daring, semi-abstract designs, based on free-flowing lines and touched with fantasy.

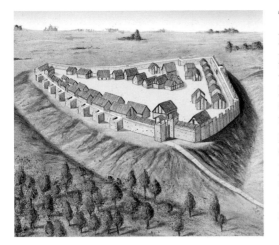

The Hallstatt chiefdoms

In the later Hallstatt centuries, better food production and increasing trade with the Mediterranean world brought greater prosperity. One sign of this was the power and wealth of the ruling class. In earlier times, chiefs were little different from other people, but by about 700 B.C., a rich ruling class, or aristocracy, had appeared. These people were the ones who controlled economic activities such as mining and trade networks. They owned slaves and lived in special forts.

Visible mounds scattered across Europe are the most obvious remains of the Hallstatt Celts. Warfare was common, and hill-forts, with fortifications of earth and timber (left), provided refuge for people who lived on nearby farms.

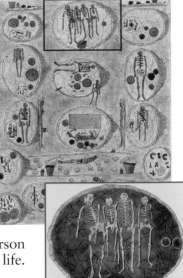

Burials

While peasants were cremated, their rulers were buried with great ceremony in wooden tombs under an earthen mound, or "barrow." Rulers were carried to their tombs on beautifully made carts pulled by horses, and the carts (and sometimes horses, too) were buried with them. The Celts believed in a life after death much like this one, so they also placed weapons and other articles—including valuable, Greek-made vessels—in the tomb. Sometimes they put in a joint of pork, so the dead person would not go hungry on the way to the next life.

The painting above shows the structure of graves at Hallstatt found by archaeologists about 150 years ago. Inset: detail of Celtic skeletons in a grave.

Miners at Hallstatt used these rucksacks, made of leather stiffened with strips of wood, to carry the salt. Thanks to the salty surroundings, the rucksacks look almost new 2,000 years later.

The Celtic World

Great disturbances took place in the Celtic world in the fourth and fifth centuries B.C. They marked the end of the old Hallstatt aristocracy and the beginning of the La Tène culture, which gradually replaced the Hallstatt in most Celtic lands. These changes may have caused great migrations, which carried the Celts across Europe. Early tribal peoples often moved into new areas in search of more land or to escape an invasion. The ancestors of the Celts themselves probably came from farther east. Already present in southern Britain and northern Spain by 500 B.C., Celts spread throughout Scotland, Ireland, and the Iberian peninsula. Others crossed the Alps into northern Italy, attacking Rome in about 387 B.C. By 300 B.C., other tribal groups had settled in the Ukraine. Celts raided deep into Greece in 279 B.C. and made settlements around the Black Sea. One group turned east and crossed the Bosphorus to settle in Galatia, central Turkey.

Head of a man, from about 100 B.C., found in Bohemia, the home of some of the invaders of the Balkans. The swept-back hair and big moustache fit the descriptions of Celtic men in western Europe, too.

NORTH SEA

La Tène

GAUL

Hallstatt

IBERIA

Rome
ITALY

BLACK SEA

Delphi

MEDITERRANEAN SEA

ANATOLIA

From Greece to Anatolia

The attack on Greece in 279 B.C. was one of the last, and least successful, Celtic invasions. The raiders attacked the sacred city of Delphi, where the Greek cities stored their treasure, but they were soon driven off. One small group founded the short-lived kingdom of Tylis, on the Black Sea. Another, larger group, the future Galatians, was invited to settle permanently in central Anatolia by local rulers who hoped to employ the Celts as soldiers.

What caused the migrations of the Celts? A Greek writer said they wanted more land and closer trade with the Mediterranean, but they may have had other reasons, too.

The craftsmanship of this bronze wine jug (right), made about 350 B.C., is Celtic, but the style and decoration show Etruscan influence.

Italy

Celts from Gaul crossed the Alps about 400 B.C., and fought with the Etruscans, then the dominant people in Italy. In 387 B.C., the Celts attacked Rome, before settling in the north. Their La Tène culture was influenced by Etruscan customs, and they were the first Celtic peoples to live in towns. In 283 B.C., they suffered their first defeat by the Romans: within a century, they fell under Roman control.

Gaul

Gaul, or Gallia, was the Roman name for the region between the river Rhine and the Pyrenees. By about 400 B.C., all the Gauls belonged to the La Tène culture. The Romans took over the southwest in the second century B.C., and contact with the Mediterranean partly "Romanized" the Gauls before Julius Caesar conquered the whole country in the 50s B.C.

Decorated bronze mirrors were popular in Britain in the first century A.D. This one shows the bold, imaginative designs, based on flowing lines, of the La Tène culture.

The Gauls, imitating the Greeks, began to produce their own gold and silver coins before 200 B.C. Coins bore lively artistic designs of horses, chariots, and other animals.

Britain and Ireland

The Celts of Britain and Ireland were different from those of mainland Europe. They saw themselves as a separate people, although in language and culture they were like their neighbors in Gaul. Three peoples lived in Britain: the Britons in the south, the Caledonians north of the Forth-Clyde rivers, and the Hibernians in Ireland. Their languages were quite closely related.

The Celtiberians

The Celts who settled in Spain and Portugal mixed with the native people, the Iberians. The language remained Celtic, but in many ways—clothes, weapons, art—Celtiberian culture was different from both the Hallstatt and La Tène.

Religion

The Celts were a very religious people, although they had no organized church. Like Hindus, or ancient Romans, the Celts had many gods and goddesses, but most were local. The Celts believed the gods were their ancestors, not their creators. A tribal god and goddess were the "father" and "mother" of the tribe. As in other religions, the gods behaved like humans (sometimes badly) but had superhuman powers. People made offerings to them, including human sacrifice, at shrines. Many other things were sacred—certain animals, rivers, springs, forest clearings—or had some supernatural meaning. The number three was lucky, and images of gods sometimes appeared in threes. The Celts believed that the human soul was in the head, which explains their many carvings of heads or skulls and their habit of preserving the heads of enemies. A person's soul was believed to be immortal, and after death, life was thought to continue in the "Otherworld" much as before.

Rites and sacrifice

Because writing was forbidden by the druids, no one knows exactly how the Celts worshipped their gods. But it is known that they performed certain ceremonies in sacred places, shrines or sanctuaries, and, in later times, temples. Their object was to please the gods, and their ceremonies included making gifts and offering sacrifices. Both animals and human beings (usually, but not always, criminals) were sacrificed. Gifts and sacrifices have been found in deep pits, or ritual shafts, in some sanctuaries.

Some ritual shafts were up to 130 feet (40 m) deep. Their purpose was probably to make contact with the gods of the Underworld.

Gods and goddesses

Scholars know the names of more than 400 Celtic gods and goddesses, but most were probably local versions of the same god. Tribal gods were usually represented as heroic warrior-hunters, such as the horn-headed Cernunnos, who protected the tribe and brought success in the hunt. Goddesses were usually related to the Earth Mother, and their interests were the production of good crops and healthy children. Many gods were associated with special activities, such as healing, and some appear as blacksmiths or other craftsmen. The Irish goddess Flidais was connected with animals and the forest. The British goddess Sulis looked after the famous springs at Bath.

The goddess Epona, always linked with a horse, was widely known in the Celtic world. The Celts adopted some Roman gods, but Epona was the only Celtic deity adopted (as protector of cavalry) by the Romans.

Dogs were connected with healing (perhaps because they healed themselves easily by licking) and the afterlife. Dogs, usually looking something like wolfhounds, were often pictured with goddesses.

Sacred animals

The Celts believed that some animals had supernatural powers. They gave special respect to the wild boar for its strength and courage, and a boar was often shown on shields. The dog, so useful in the hunt, was another. The stag and the horse were sacred, as well as smaller creatures such as the hare and the serpent, and birds such as the raven and the swan.

This god (left) wearing a helmet mounted with antlers is Cernunnos, the chief Celtic god, usually shown wearing horns or antlers. He was known in Britain and mainland Europe and may have been the same as the Irish Dagda ("the capable god").

A votive offering of a model boat, made of gold in the first century B.C. It was found in Ireland and shows that Celtic boats had sails, perhaps the first in northern Europe, as well as oars.

This temple belongs to the Roman period, but it is an advanced version of an older Celtic temple, such as one discovered at Heathrow Airport, London. Temple precincts (surroundings) were enclosed by a fence and a ditch.

Votive offerings

Votive offerings were gifts to the gods. Many of the finest works of Celtic craftsmanship found by archaeologists are votive offerings. After a victory in battle, warriors would present their weapons to the gods, throwing them into a sacred spot in a river or lake. Sacred sites and temples became treasuries of sorts, filled with gold and silver. Not all gifts were so valuable. People seeking cures offered a wood carving of a human figure, or the part of the body that needed healing.

Sacred places

There were many places where the Celts went to worship their gods. Although they later built wooden temples, the Celts used mostly natural places (with no man-made additions) that had some striking feature, such as a spring, unusual rock formation, hilltop, or clearing in the forest. The popular idea of a sacred grove, as described by Roman writers, was a space surrounded by oak trees growing mistletoe, a sacred plant, which was cut from the tree by a white-robed druid with a golden hook.

A great river such as the Seine, flowing for nearly 500 miles (800 km) through Gaul, begins as a trickle of water from a spring. To the Celts, these springs were magical, becoming shrines where people made offerings, perhaps throwing gold coins into the water.

The Druids

The Celtic religious authorities were the druids, who presided over all religious worship and ceremonies. They were greatly respected and were thought to have supernatural powers: they could foretell the future, or turn themselves (and other people) into animals. They were the wise men of society, not only priests but also judges, teachers, and healers. They were superior to all others, except perhaps kings and rulers. The highest class of this intellectual elite were the priestly druids. Second came the vates, including augurs, who foretold the future from signs, and third were the bards, or poet-historians. The Celts were divided into many tribes, but the druids stood above tribal society. They could prevent wars and get hostile tribes to act together. But because Celtic languages were not written, we know very little about the druids, except from the reports of the Romans, their enemies.

The name "druid" may mean "knowledge of the oak." The sacred groves of the druids were often clearings among oak trees, especially if mistletoe was present. Mistletoe was supposed to be a healing plant, and it probably played a part in religious ceremony.

An arch-druid, chief of the druids, giving his judgment as "chief justice." Artists have to rely on their imagination because no one knows how druids dressed, though some Roman writers mention white robes.

Priests

Druids directed all religious rituals and worship, and also instructed people in the mysteries of the heavens and the powers of the gods. An important part of religion was sacrifice, of animals and human beings. Sacrifices pleased the gods and therefore promoted fertility—good harvests, healthy babies, and farm animals. The augurs were also able to predict future events by such signs as the movements of a dying man. Because the Celts believed that life went on after death, human sacrifice seemed less dreadful to them.

This stone carving from Gaul, made about 200 B.C., shows a monster eating a human being, with its claws on two tasty heads. It represents the grim side of Celtic belief.

Becoming a druid

Young people were eager to become druids because druids enjoyed many privileges, such as freedom from taxes and military service. However, the training was long and hard. Among other things, it required great powers of memory, since there were no books. To reach the highest class of priestly druids took up to 20 years. Other classes needed fewer—12 years for the second class (augurs), only 7 for a bard. Training took place in remote places, for the druids were anxious to keep their knowledge to themselves.

This bronze headdress, found in a Celtic temple from Roman times in England, is believed to have been a druid's crown.

Judges

Quarrels between different tribes, arguments about property, and crimes such as theft or murder, if they were not solved by fighting, were subject to the judgment of the druids. Important matters were decided at the annual gathering of the druids, which in Gaul took place southwest of modern Paris. Those who refused the druids' judgment were outlawed from sacrifice—a dreadful fate, like being exiled from life itself.

Druidesses

Women were found in all classes of Celtic society, including rulers. Stories exist of witches, such as the Nine Witches of Gloucester in an old Welsh tale, and priestesses, as well as women who had the same authority as male druids in both religion and politics, deciding on peace or war. Other women could foretell the future and cure sickness. Old Irish legends mention many women with supernatural powers.

Left: A female figure, probably a goddess, attended by priestesses, or female druids, from the silver Gundestrup cauldron.

Keepers of the sacred lore

All the learned classes were masters of poetry, especially the bards. They composed and memorized long "praise-poems," celebrating the deeds of rulers and heroes. They sang these poems accompanied by a lyre (a stringed instrument like a small harp). The poems of the bards also had magic power, bringing benefits to the tribe. The bards continued well into Christian times (mainly as entertainers), with the lucky result that some of their tales were written down by Irish (and some Welsh) monks.

Sculpture of a bard with his lyre. From the bards, much is known about heroes such as Cú Chulainn, though the Irish monks who wrote the stories down may have made changes to suit Christian beliefs.

It was said that in the first century B.C., an order of priestesses lived by themselves on an island in the river Loire, where they had a sanctuary, or temple, a very early example of a religious building. Every year the sisters re-thatched the temple roof in a special ceremony and consecrated it by sacrificing one of themselves. The victim was the one who dropped her bundle of reeds (perhaps because she was pushed). In a religious frenzy, her sisters tore her to pieces.

Burial

The most useful evidence of the Celts' way of life comes from graves and cemeteries. Because the Celts believed that life continued after death, graves were filled with possessions that the dead person might need, including jewelry, weapons, tools, cooking pots, and even food and drink. These things provide clues to everyday life. Modern scientific methods can extract even more clues from human remains, including what people ate, or what diseases they suffered from. It is sometimes even possible to "rebuild" their faces. The Celts treated funerals as grand ceremonies. The more important the dead person, the grander the ceremony, with a procession and feasting, and the larger the tomb. The mound covering the burial chamber of one great Celtic chieftain was 200 feet (60 m) across.

The tomb chambers of people of the highest rank were covered by a mound, or barrow, made of soil covered with turf.

Grave goods

The goods that filled the burial chambers of the rich and powerful sometimes included the funeral cart or chariot that had brought the body to the tomb, and perhaps the dead warrior's horse and other animals. According to Julius Caesar (first century B.C.), in Gaul, a man's favorite slaves or servants were often sacrificed with him.

One of the richest graves discovered so far was of a woman, at Vix (France). Among the grave goods was this giant bronze vessel for wine—it holds 286 gallons (1,100 l).

This stone figure may represent a ruler, or perhaps Cernunnos, the horned god of the dead, who was known throughout most of the Celtic world. The statue was found recently in southern Germany. It is 6 feet (1.8 m) tall and weighs about 500 pounds (230 kg). It may have stood on top of a burial mound.

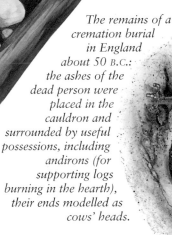

The remains of a cremation burial in England about 50 B.C.: the ashes of the dead person were placed in the cauldron and surrounded by useful possessions, including andirons (for supporting logs burning in the hearth), their ends modelled as cows' heads.

Bog burials

Swamps and marshes were more common in Europe 2,000 years ago, and the Celts threw treasure into them, probably as offerings to the gods. Human bodies have also been found in bogs: they may have been sacrificed for the same reason. A famous example is Lindow Man, found near Manchester, England, in 1984. The peat bog had preserved his body, including skin and fingernails. He had been executed about A.D. 100, and his stomach contained traces of mistletoe, the sacred plant of the druids.

The body of Lindow Man was naked. He had been hit with an axe, then strangled with a cord. Finally, his throat was cut, and he was thrown, face down, into Lindow Marsh.

Cremation

By the first century B.C., grand burials were less common, and the rich funeral ceremonies of earlier times disappeared throughout much of the Celtic world. Most people were now cremated (their bodies burned). Sometimes the ashes were put in a pit, or in a wooden bucket or large pot, before being buried. Cemeteries with hundreds of such graves have been found. Other European peoples, including the Romans, also practiced cremation, as did the ancestors of the Celts, 1,000 years earlier.

The Celts admired the wild boar above all other animals for its strength and courage. The boar was a dangerous quarry, even for skilled horsemen such as the Celtiberians.

Farming and Food

Celtic towns did not exist until after 100 B.C., and even in later times most people lived in farms and small villages. Celtic legends may be full of heroes and battles, but growing food was the main occupation of most people. Poor harvests or disease sometimes brought disaster, but in general, the Celts were very successful farmers. They were able to grow enough to export products to other regions, as well as to feed the smaller numbers of people— warrior-nobles, craftsmen, priests—who were not farmers. Life in the country meant more than tending crops and herds. Many other tasks were involved, such as maintaining the water supply, digging storage pits, making fences, and managing the surrounding woodlands that provided timber for building and fuel.

Hunting and fishing

In most regions, wild animals provided much of the meat supply, along with fish caught in nets, shellfish gathered on the seashore, and birds caught in traps. The Celts hunted animals for food, but hunting was also, if not quite a sport, a manly occupation. It provided good training for war and a way for a man to prove his courage. The wild boar, dangerous to men armed only with spears but admired for its ferocity, was a favorite quarry. Helped by hounds, hunters also killed deer and smaller animals such as hares.

Crops

The main crops were cereals: several kinds of early wheat, with smaller ears than modern varieties; barley, for brewing beer; millet, widely grown in Gaul; and oats and rye, grown in colder parts. Grain was milled into flour by hand when required, using heavy stones. Cereals also provided straw for animals' winter feed. The Celts grew beans, peas, and other vegetables. They gathered honey as well as certain edible green plants, especially the common weed called "fat hen," from the wild.

The common breed of sheep was a tough, goat-like animal with a coarse fleece, rather like the wild Soay sheep that still live in the Hebrides. They provided chiefly wool, sometimes milk, and perhaps meat when they were old.

This rock carving shows a man guiding a plow drawn by a pair of oxen. This early plow, wooden with an iron tip, broke up but did not turn the soil. It cut deep, turning up big clods, which were then broken up by men with mattocks or hoes.

Farm animals

The Celts loved horses, which they used in war and for transport. Oxen did the heavier work on the farm. Like all farm animals, cattle were smaller than modern breeds but strong and hardy. Pigs, which partly fed themselves by foraging, provided a favorite meat. Domestic pigs looked, and perhaps tasted, like their wild cousins. Chickens were kept for eggs and meat, dogs for hunting, guarding property, and as pets. Besides meat, animals provided important materials such as bone, horn, leather, and skins.

The Celts made their own cookware. Some implements were just like those used today. The spit (above) has hook rings decorated with birds. The big double-hook was for lifting pieces of meat from the simmering cauldron.

Storing food

A big problem for people living in cold climates is providing food for the winter. The Celts preserved meat in several ways, for instance by salting it or by hanging it high above the hearth, where it would be smoked. Grain and dried vegetables had to be processed and stored where rodents and other pests could not get at them, in granaries raised above the ground on stilts, or in pits. For everyday storage, the Celts used mainly jars and bowls of pottery (right), which they made themselves, though rich people owned imported vessels.

Cooking food

Cooking was done over the hearth in the center of the main (often only) room. Meat was roasted on a spit, or stewed, along with vegetables, in a cauldron which hung permanently on a chain from the roof, or from a tripod. Cauldrons, which could also be used for brewing beer, had a special importance for the Celts. Some have been found made of gold: they probably played a part in religious rituals. Bread was baked in an oven. The hearth was the central point of feasts. Sometimes the food was placed on low wooden tables, while everyone sat on skins on the ground around the hearth.

The Celts had their own way of storing large amounts of grain for a long time. They dug pits in the ground, up to 6.5 feet (2 m) deep, filled them, and sealed them with clay or animal dung. Grain on the very top and edges germinated, using up the oxygen and replacing it with carbon dioxide, which prevented further germination. Grain stored in this way lasted six months, longer if necessary.

The Celts at War

Carrying arms and demonstrating courage and bravery were important symbols of manhood among the Celts, and war was the perfect opportunity to show these qualities. In early times, the Celts fought among themselves—resolving family feuds and forging new tribal relationships—as well as against the peoples they encountered as they spread across Europe. In Roman times, they amassed huge armies in an attempt to defeat the expanding Roman Empire. However, they were no match for the well-armed and disciplined troops from Rome and were soon subdued.

This Roman statue of a Celtic warrior shows why these men were feared.

Celtic sword and thrusting knife.

Weapons

Celtic warriors all carried a long spear and a shield. Wealthier Celts would also have carried a sword and worn a protective metal helmet and a shirt of chain mail. The Celts also used bows and arrows and slings in battle.

Celtic statue of a foot soldier.

Cavalry and foot soldiers

As the use of chariots declined around 200 B.C., more and more Celtic warriors fought from horseback. They had special four-pommelled saddles which allowed them to fight effectively while mounted, even though they did not use stirrups. The beautiful riding horses of Gaul and Spain made excellent warhorses.

Until about 200 B.C., many Celtic warriors fought naked. They decorated their bodies with tattoos and carried only their weapons.

Battle tactics

When the Celts were face to face with their enemies, they formed a line of battle, grouped by clan. Sometimes, prominent warriors challenged the foes' leaders to hand-to-hand combat before the main battle began. Meanwhile, the rest of the warriors worked themselves into a frenzy with battle songs, chants, and horn playing, often drinking large amounts of alcohol. They made a tremendous din before hurling themselves at their enemy (who sometimes fled in terror before the fighting even began).

Chariots

Early Celtic armies were composed of large numbers of chariots. These were single-axled vehicles, drawn by two ponies, that carried a driver and a warrior. They raced about the field even before the battle began, creating vast amounts of noise and uproar to dishearten opponents.

This coin shows a Celtic warrior terrorizing the enemy in his war chariot.

Warriors

The Celts used no armor at all until about 300 B.C., when they invented chain mail (which the Romans soon copied). However, a suit of chain mail was very expensive, and only aristocratic warriors, such as the one shown here, could afford one. Most warriors fought in breeches and shirt.

"On their heads they wear bronze helmets which possess large projecting fingers lending the appearance of enormous stature to their wearer." Greek historian Diodorus Siculus

This illustration shows Roman soldiers being attacked by Celts in a war chariot.

Society and Daily Life

Most Celtic societies appear to have been hierarchical, or pyramid-shaped, with a king at the top who delegated a part of his power to a small group of warrior aristocrats in return for their loyalty. The aristocrats ruled over the vast majority of people, who were almost all farmers. There were a few other groups within Celtic society, such as soldiers, craftworkers, bards, and druids. The other main division in Celtic societies was between men and women. In general, women's lives revolved around their families. Women raised children, prepared food, spun wool, and wove cloth to make into clothing. They also did a lot of farm work. Their lives were probably hard, and there is some evidence to suggest that many Celtic women died younger than their menfolk.

This face was carved in England after the Roman invasion. It shows a Roman gorgon figure, but with a typical Celtic moustache and hair.

This bronze statue is thought to show a Celtic god. He has blue eyes and a toned, muscular body. He is also wearing a gold torque around his neck.

Celtic men

"The Gauls are tall of body, with rippling muscles, and white of skin, and their hair is blond. . . ."
This is how the Greek historian Diodorus Siculus described Celtic men in the first century B.C. Greek and Roman writers were struck by the Celts' appearance, commenting in detail on the large moustaches worn by noblemen and their chalked, spiky hair.

Small societies and kinship

Most Celts lived in small settlements, sometimes consisting of just a farmhouse or two, or a fortified towerhouse (such as the broch shown below). These groups generally consisted of extended families and clans, and their slaves. These sub-tribes, which the Romans called pagi, were united in larger tribal units, usually under a king or chief. Sometimes several tribes joined together to form a confederation, but these groupings were generally short-lived.

This illustration shows what a Scottish broch would have looked like in the first century B.C. Brochs were occupied by a single family and had a large central living area surrounded by sleeping alcoves.

Writing

The first Celtic societies did not use a written language. They had a very strong oral culture, and many Celts were excellent speakers. After they came into contact with societies that did have written languages, such as the Greeks, they also began to write, mainly for administrative purposes.

A Celtic inscription carved into a stone.

Clothing

Celtic men wore long trousers called breeches, and long-sleeved tunics or shirts. In cold weather they also wore woolen cloaks with tartan patterns or tweedy textures. The women wore long dresses, often with colored shawls wrapped over their shoulders. Their dresses were fastened at the shoulders with a pair of pins.

Childhood

Celtic children did not go to school. They stayed at home and learned how to become farmers and housewives from their parents. Many young men became soldiers and travelled far from home.

This glass drinking cup was found in France. Even though it is made of delicate material, it is thought to have been used to feed a child too young to drink from a cup.

Celtic weavers used upright weighted looms such as the one shown here. Once the cloth was spun and woven, it was made into clothing. Celtic women were responsible for all of these tasks.

Women's lives

Most Celtic women lived traditional lives, busily raising their children and taking care of their homes. Some historians believe that they enjoyed a little more freedom and power than Greek or Roman women. Some noblewomen, such as Boudicca (see page 37), were directly involved in political issues and conflict.

This skull was found in Austria. It shows how a Celtic surgeon drilled a hole through the bone to the brain.

Health

The Celts tried to cure many ailments with herbal medicines and by appealing to supernatural powers. However, they also used special saws and drills to perform sophisticated brain surgery.

Celtic Homesteads

Most Celts lived on the land and worked as farmers. They lived in farmsteads, or hamlets consisting of just a few houses. Each farmhouse was home to an extended family and their servants, as well as their farm animals and pets.

The Celts lived in the cooler climates of Europe and Britain. They did not leave an open smoke hole in their roofs. The smoke just filtered through the thatch.

Food

The Celts grew the food they needed in the fields around their homes. Their main cereal crops were barley, oats, wheat, and rye. They also grew vegetables: beans, peas, onions, and lentils. They kept pigs for their meat and sheep for their wool and milk. Cattle also provided milk, as well as meat and hides to make into leather. Geese and hens provided feathers and eggs, and bees were a source of honey, which was used as a sweetener.

Celtic houses had a wooden frame that was covered in wattle, daub, and thatch. This man is putting the finishing touches on a thatched roof.

1. STOREROOM
2. THATCHED ROOF
3. SLEEPING QUARTERS
4. HEARTH
5. LOOM, FOR WEAVING
6. BARRELS FOR STORING FOODSTUFFS
7. WOODEN FRAME
8. ENTRANCE
9. CHILDREN PLAYING
10. ADULTS DOING CHORES
11. FARM ANIMALS IN ENCLOSED AREAS

At the time of the Celts, Europe and Britain had far more woodlands than today. The Celts were fine hunters, supplementing their farm-based diet with wild animals and fish. These men (left) have caught a wild boar for their dinner.

Many basic farm tools and household utensils were made by the farmers themselves or by village blacksmiths. These tools were used to cut cereal crops.

Celtic women were responsible for household chores and also for spinning and weaving clothing for the entire family.

Celtic farmhouses

For most Celts, life was centered on the home—one big room in which all the family members ate, slept, and did their daily chores. An open fire in the middle of the room provided light and heat, and was also used for cooking. One important daily task was grinding grain into flour to make bread. Grain was also used to make porridge and beer, both of which were important in the diet. Stews and roast meat were also eaten.

The main house was surrounded by smaller buildings, including the storeroom and various shelters for animals and implements. Water was usually brought from a nearby river or spring and stored in barrels or cisterns.

Technology

The Celts were expert craftsmen, good at making things. They were especially skillful in metals, mainly bronze during most of the Hallstatt culture, and iron increasingly from about 700 B.C. Of course, metal objects (especially gold) last longer than materials such as wood, leather, or cloth, so more is known about them, but clearly other Celtic craftspeople, such as carpenters or weavers, were equally skillful. The Celts were not as good at large engineering projects, partly because they were not good at making long-term plans or working together on long-term projects. They seldom used stone, although there were exceptions, such as the round tower-houses, called brochs, in northern Scotland. They did dig deep and complicated mines (see page 8) and, although only a few traces of their roads have survived (preserved in bogs), laid long wooden trackways to carry their carts over marshy ground.

This helmet is steel, but the hawk (which has wings that flap) on top is bronze. People did not stop making bronze when they learned how to make iron. While iron was best for swords, bronze was better for decorative objects.

This is a reconstruction of a war chariot found in a grave from the first century B.C. in Wales. The inner, wooden rim of each wheel is made from a single strip of wood, strengthened by an iron clamp where the two ends meet.

Glass

The Celts knew how to make glass by about 500 B.C., and soon afterwards the first full-time glassmaking workshops appeared. Glass was chiefly used for decoration—jewelry, ornaments (such as the little dog on page 28), and the eyes for carved heads. Celtic glassworkers could not make clear glass, nor could they "blow" glass to make large vessels, until Roman times.

This owl-like cup in multi-colored glass, from a grave in Romania, shows that Celtic glassmakers had a sense of humor as well as skill.

The wheel

Early wooden wheels were made out of planks shaped into a circle, but by about 300 B.C., the Celts had perfected the spoked, iron-rimmed, wooden wheel, no different from a modern cart wheel. Iron tires, when first used, were nailed on. But the Celts soon learned that iron expanded when heated, and therefore heated the iron tire before fitting it. As the tire cooled, it gripped more tightly.

Gold and silver

The most spectacular objects that have survived from Celtic times are made of gold or silver. An amazing number of gold objects were buried in graves or as offerings during the period of rich warrior-chiefs (about 700–400 B.C.).

Torques are the best-known products of Celtic goldsmiths. A torque was a kind of necklace of plaited gold wire, worn by the rich elite (men and women). It may have been attributed magical qualities. This magnificent example was found in Norfolk, England.

Celtic craftsmen used enamel, glass fused to metal, to decorate the bronze fittings on horse harnesses.

Bronze and iron

People of the Hallstatt culture were skillful workers in bronze, an alloy of copper and tin. Bronze could be cast in a mold, formed into thin sheets, or decorated in many ways—by hammering, engraving, piercing, etc. It was hard-wearing and did not rust. Iron, which first appeared around the eighth century B.C., was harder to make and needed higher temperatures. But iron had many advantages over bronze, especially for tools and weapons. It was stronger, harder, and provided a sharp cutting edge.

Metalworking became a specialized business, and tribes that controlled a big deposit of iron ore grew rich through trade. In other places, local groups still produced just enough metal for their own needs. The man on the right is fitting an iron tip to a plowshare. His companion pours molten bronze into a mold.

Blacksmiths

Blacksmiths, who made useful tools and weapons from raw metal, seemed to have almost magical ability. They belonged to the elite class and commanded great respect.

A cauldron was the centerpiece of every house. This bronze cauldron (left) of about 700 B.C. is in such good condition that it was probably made for special ceremonies only. In later times, cauldrons were usually made of iron. The iron fork is for spearing meat in the cauldron, and the knife is for cutting the meat.

Art

Celtic art has been described as "one of the greatest glories of prehistoric Europe." The Celtic style is not realistic, like the art of Greece and Rome. It is based on free-flowing, curving lines that form lively and beautiful patterns. Although it pictures animals, objects, and, less often, people, it is not interested in strict accuracy. This "curvilinear" ("curving-line") style, unique to the Celts, applies both to flat surfaces and objects in three dimensions. The style was based partly on their own traditions and partly on the art of other peoples, mainly the Greeks and Romans, whom the Celts came to know through trade. The Celts did not paint large pictures and seldom made free-standing sculptures. With their keen sense of design, they loved to decorate even humble objects—weapons, tools, cooking pots, harnesses, coins, mirrors, combs, and jewelry.

The beauty of this horse's head, in gold, lies in its simplicity. With just two curving lines, two circles (nostrils), and two slits (eyes), it is not just a horse, but a weary one, a horse feeling sorry for itself. Horses were a favorite subject in Celtic art. They were often associated with the goddess Epona, and this horse may be intended to represent her.

Glassmakers' workshops existed as early as the fourth century B.C. Among their products were jewelry, beads, and ornaments such as the odd little dog shown left above. The dog was made by spinning different-colored strands of half-melted glass around a stick. The Celts seem to have been especially fond of blue and white or blue and yellow.

This group of statues was found in a grave from the seventh century B.C. in Austria. It is part of a larger group, with many figures of men, women, horses, and stags, forming a procession. They are carrying the soul of the dead person to the Otherworld. At the center of the group is the tall figure of a goddess.

This beautiful gold bowl, found in a grave in Germany, dates from the early La Tène period, when the Celtic "curvilinear" style was just developing. It is a wonderful piece of Celtic craftsmanship, but the design shows influence from the Mediterranean. This must be the result of trade, perhaps via the Greek merchants based at Massalia (Marseille).

Pottery

People had made pots and cups from baked clay for centuries. By about 500 B.C., Celtic potters were making shapely pots on a wheel, which were then fired (baked) in a kiln (oven). Potters, who originally made pottery in villages for local use, soon moved into professional workshops and made pots for export. The potters had many techniques for decorating their ware—cutting patterns in the clay with a stick or a bone, or even a finger, and painting with thin, liquid clay in different colors.

Here, one man is painting a wine jar before firing, while another grinds pigment to color the clay. In the background is the kiln, which was designed so that the flow of oxygen could be controlled, allowing variations in the final color.

This pottery jug (below) was found in Numantia, northern Spain. It was made about 100 B.C. The Celts who settled in Spain before 500 B.C. mingled with the native people, the Iberians, and the culture and styles of art that developed were different from the La Tène culture of most of the Celtic world.

Jewelry

A great deal of Celtic jewelry has survived, partly because it was made of materials that do not rot, and because it was often placed in graves, where it was fairly safe. The Celts loved fine jewelry, and the goldsmiths of the La Tène culture were as skilled as those of any later time, up to the 18th century.

Gold, which was found more widely in Celtic times, was used in jewelry by those who could afford it, both men and women. Beads were made from colored glass, coral, amber, and other materials.

Festivals

The Celts enjoyed parties, and there are many accounts of lively feasts where barrels of wine and beer were drunk. Feasts helped to bring the tribe together and also established a man's status. The greatest warrior received the best cut of meat, and the question of who was the bravest was settled by mock fights, or sometimes real ones. One Irish feast ended with a pile of corpses! Feasts were local affairs, but the four great festivals that marked the changing seasons were held all over the Celtic world. Some lasted for weeks and, besides eating and drinking, included games and sporting contests such as horse racing. But, besides entertainment, festivals were important religious ceremonies, directed by the druids, and sometimes also political assemblies.

This modern illustration of the Celtic year, which began in November, shows the seasons and festivals of the Celtic calendar. The calendar was calculated by the druids. It was divided into 12 months, measured by the moon (each 29 or 30 nights). As 12 of the moon's months are less than the sun's year, an extra month of 30 days was added every three years to make up the time.

Dis Pater (left), father of the gods and therefore also the ancestor of kings, who were supposed to be descended from gods. Samhain was the season during which, people believed, the boundaries between them and the gods, and between this world and the Otherworld, vanished.

Samhain

Samhain was one of the two most important annual festivals. It marked the Celtic New Year, November 1, when the warm, light season ended, and the cold, dark season began. It was an ominous time, when many events in Celtic myth, such as the great battle of the gods in Ireland, were supposed to have happened. On Samhain eve (October 31), gods moved mysteriously among the people, playing cruel tricks on them, and the druids' magic was needed against ghostly visitors from the Otherworld. (Samhain is probably the origin of Halloween.)

Imbolc

Imbolc was one of the two lesser festivals. It was held on the eve and day of February 1 and marked the time when pregnant animals, such as sheep and cows, began to produce milk in preparation for the birth of their lambs and calves. The festival was linked with a mother-goddess who was known in Ireland as Brigid. Daughter of a druid named Dubthach, she became a popular saint in Christian times.

An image of Brigantia, British version of Brigid, whom the Romans linked with Minerva—like Brigid, a goddess of crafts. A fire burned permanently at Brigid's shrine (later a monastery) in Kildare, which was guarded by 19 maidens. No man was allowed near.

Lughnasa

The third festival of the year was generally known as Lughnasa (the Coligny calendar calls it Rivros), after the popular god Lugh, who was known in all parts of the Celtic world. It was held in July and August, and celebrated the start of the harvest. It was also the time when many tribes gathered together. Besides serious meetings and trials, contests and entertainment took place, as well as heavy drinking.

The Coligny calendar

These precious fragments found at Coligny (Gaul) are some of the earliest-known records written in a Celtic language, although the letters are Roman. The fragments come from a bronze panel made after Caesar's conquest of Gaul, probably by a druid. Covering a period of five years, the calendar names the months and festivals. Some months are marked MAT (good, or lucky) and some ANM (bad).

A stone head from Roman Britain of the god Mabon, or Maponus. His name means "son," and he was a god of youth, of poetry, and a hunter. He may appear, under another name, in The Mabinogion, *the famous collection of early Welsh tales.*

Beltane

The major festivals, Beltane and Samhain, marked the division of the year into dark and light seasons. Beltane fell on May 1, the beginning of summer. Like Samhain, Beltane was believed to be an eventful, perhaps dangerous, time, when great events, good or bad, took place. Sacrifices of animals, and perhaps humans too, were necessary to protect crops and livestock. Beltane was strongly associated with fire, a magical force that, like water, was revered by the druids.

The druids carried out a ceremony during Beltane in which they forced cattle to pass between two fires. It was meant to protect the animals from disease. As "Beltane" comes from words meaning "good luck," this ceremony may have given the festival its name.

Beltane

Villages and Towns

Most Celts lived in small villages or sometimes single farmsteads housing one large, extended family. These farming settlements produced almost everything—clothes, food, shelter—that people needed. What they could not provide was safety against attack, and in violent times, the people from the villages and farms took shelter, with their animals, in a well-protected hill-fort. By about 100 B.C., society had settled down. Trade increased, crafts became more specialized, and the Celtic world came under the influence of Mediterranean civilization, where city life had existed for centuries. The result was the development of Celtic *oppida*, the Latin (Roman) word for "towns."

Brochs

A broch is a round tower house built of stone, without mortar. It was a type of family fortress common in northern Scotland between 600 B.C. and A.D. 200. Some had walls 16 feet (5 m) thick and 49 feet (15 m) high, getting narrower as they went up, for extra strength. A narrow staircase inside the wall led to a gallery, where the chief's family was safe from almost any attack.

Hill-forts

The outstanding monuments left by the Celts were hill-forts. Hundreds can still be seen across Europe. They had many uses, but the main one was defense. Some had no permanent residents but were used for safe storage and as a refuge in time of war. They were defended by huge ramparts of earth supported by timber and stone. Maiden Castle, in southern Britain, has four rings of ramparts, with ditches up to 66 feet (20 m) deep between them. The area inside covers 44 acres (18 ha). The entrance to a hill-fort, being the weakest point, had extra protection.

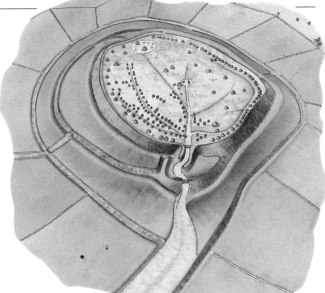

Oppida

Like hill-forts, the early Celtic towns had many different purposes, one of which was defense. Most were built in a secure place, such as the bend in a river, and had strong walls and ramparts. The growth of large, professional workshops, and therefore of trade, was another common reason for their development. Towns had well-planned streets, with houses, probably shops, a wide range of industry or crafts, perhaps a market place, and even a temple. Some were, in effect, capital cities, the center of tribal government, with a mint that made coins stamped with the king's head. In other ways, Celtic towns were unlike modern towns, and they usually contained much open land, where animals grazed.

Fun and Games

Today, people's lives are divided into separate activities, such as work and play, school and vacation. Ancient peoples did not make such clear divisions between activities. Hunting, for example, is today considered a sport. But was it a sport for the Celts? Or was it done for food? Or as a form of training for warriors? All three reasons probably played a part. Even games had a religious meaning. When studying the everyday life of the Celts, it is important to remember that the Celtic world was changing over the centuries, and that it included many different peoples with different customs. The Celtic people didn't call themselves "Celts." Nor did they think of themselves as "Gauls," "Caledonians," or "Britons." The largest unit they felt they belonged to was what people today call a "tribe."

The Celts were beer drinkers, but they proved to be equally fond of wine, served in wine jugs such as these. Strange as it seems now, there were no vineyards in Gaul, and wine was imported from the Mediterranean. Ordinary people probably could not afford it.

Feasting and banquets

The Celts were good at enjoying themselves and held many feasts or banquets. A great deal of beer and wine was drunk, and several kinds of meat were eaten, perhaps with bread and vegetables. A feast was nothing like a state banquet today. Guests sprawled on the ground and made a lot of noise. According to a Roman writer, table manners were shocking (though of course there were usually no tables!), and violent quarrels were common. Like other activities, feasts were not just entertainment. Stories of heroes past and present, recited by a bard, helped to strengthen the confidence of the whole group.

Among the musical instruments of the Celts were very long, bronze horns, or trumpets—hard to blow, but capable of making a great noise. They were probably used on special, ceremonial occasions. The Celts blew similar instruments before battle.

Music

Besides horns and drums, the Celts had a number of musical instruments, including Pan's pipes (far left) and the lyre, one of the earliest stringed instruments. These instruments were the tools of the trade of the bards (see page 15), forerunners of the travelling minstrels of the Middle Ages, who played them to accompany their poems and stories. Some of the stories still exist, but no one knows exactly what the music sounded like.

This figure of a man or god riding on a fish is part of the decoration of the silver Gundestrup cauldron. It probably illustrates an incident in Celtic myth and may represent the journey to the Otherworld, which was thought to lie across the sea to the west.

Legends

Like most people who depend on themselves to provide entertainment, the Celts loved stories, especially on the long, dark winter evenings. Although the Celts did not write them down, many colorful legends and folk tales of the ancient Celts from Ireland still exist. These tales were handed down by word of mouth over the centuries, well into Christian times. From about the eighth century, they were recorded in writing by Irish monks.

These attractive glass marbles or gaming pieces were probably counters used in a game similar to the game known in Britain as ludo. Gambling may have been involved.

Outdoor games

For the ruling class in Celtic society, warfare was an honorable activity, and most non-Celtic writers noted how quick the Celts were to start a fight. It is possible that they had some form of sporting combat, like jousting in medieval times, that was partly a sport, a way for a warrior to display his skill and bravery. Hunting, too, must have served the same purpose. Athletic contests at festivals demonstrated the strength and agility of young men.

Indoor games

Celtic children, like all other children, certainly played games, though only a few clues exist as to what they were. Children seldom appear in Celtic art, and archaeologists have found no certain examples of their toys, unless some of the small "ornaments"—for instance, of dogs—were toys. The Celts played board games, because some dice made of bone and counters in sets of four or six have been found, as has at least one example of a board for a game.

All the Celtic peoples were skilled horsemen. Unlike the Romans, most Celts liked to fight on horseback, or from a horse-drawn chariot. Horses were admired as noble animals, and craftsmen lavished their skill lovingly on harness details and even made horned helmets for them. Horse racing and chariot racing took place at the seasonal festivals in Ireland, but these activities were not pure sport. They had other purposes and may have been connected with religious ceremonies and the horse-goddess Epona.

Celts and Romans

In the third century B.C., the Celts dominated most of Europe. Yet by A.D. 200, they had almost disappeared as a distinct people, and nearly all the old Celtic world was under Roman rule. By the fifth century A.D., when the Roman Empire crumbled, the Celts were thoroughly "Roman" in culture, and, like the Romans, they had become Christians. When Rome fell, the Celts regained their independence—for a short time. Before they could establish strong states, they were conquered by other peoples. This time the invaders came not from the south (like the Romans), but from the north. Germanic tribes, such as the Franks and Anglo-Saxons, overran most of western Europe. Celtic culture survived in a few places—Brittany, Wales, part of Scotland, and Ireland, the only country not conquered by the Romans.

Conquest of Gaul

By the first century B.C., the Celtic Gauls had been in contact with the Roman world for many generations, and as trade developed and towns grew, Gaul grew more and more like the Mediterranean world to the south. The Gauls valued independence, but they seemed bound to become subjects of Rome. When the Helvetii from Switzerland invaded Gaul in 58 B.C., they provided a reason for Julius Caesar, the Roman governor of Gallia Transalpina (Provence), to "stabilize" Gaul. After three years of cruel fighting, Caesar claimed he had conquered Gaul, but the new province was not secure until the tribal king, Vercingetorix, was defeated.

This sculpture shows a Roman horseman riding over Celtic warriors. It comes from a fortified wall that the Romans built across northern Britain to control the fierce, unconquered tribes of Caledonia (Scotland).

This fine bronze helmet, probably never used in a battle, was found in modern Bari, in Apulia, where Celtic groups may have been present as early as 350 B.C. In spite of different origins, the Celts seem to have become "Italian" quite quickly.

Head hunters

The Celts believed that a person's soul lived in his or her head, which gave the head a special, supernatural importance. A Celtic warrior would carry home the head of a defeated enemy, believing that by "owning" it he also owned some of the dead man's spirit and courage. The head was soaked in oil or preserved in some other way, and displayed with pride. The skull of one Roman, says the Roman historian Livy, was cleaned out, gilded, and used as a cup in religious ceremonies.

The importance of the head is obvious from the number of bodiless heads that appear in Celtic carvings, such as these made in southern Gaul about 200 B.C. Actual skulls have also been found, set in stone, in Celtic sanctuaries.

Barbarian Celts

In 387 B.C., the Celts raided Rome and held the place for ransom, to punish the Romans for helping the Etruscans against them. The Romans never forgot that experience, and ever afterwards they feared attack from the north by the "barbarians." That was the name Romans gave to all peoples outside their empire. It was not as rude as it sounds today, meaning only "non-Romans," but the Romans certainly believed they were superior to any barbarians. In the end, even the Celts themselves came to agree—by becoming "Romans" themselves.

Celtic presence in Italy

In the fourth century B.C., Celtic tribes from Gaul settled in the Po valley, in northern Italy, a region later called Cisalpine Gaul. Some moved farther south, along the coast of the Adriatic, and a few groups reached Apulia, in the south. At that time, the dominant Italian people were the Etruscans. In Cisalpine Gaul, the newcomers found Etruscan towns already existing, and they became the first Celtic town-dwellers. The more southerly Celts also adopted many Etruscan customs. Under the growing power of Rome, all the Italian Celts came under Roman rule by 191 B.C., and in 49 B.C., the people of Cisalpine Gaul, no longer "Celts," became Roman citizens.

The Roman empire resulted not from some great plan, but from the rivalries of ambitious men in Rome. Julius Caesar gained such power and wealth from his conquests that he became ruler of Rome, but he was assassinated in 44 B.C.

Boudicca's Revolt

Boudicca was the widow of the king of the Iceni (in eastern Britain), who died in A.D. 60. He left half his property to his daughters and half to the Roman emperor, but greedy Romans tried to take the lot. Enraged, Boudicca rebelled. Many other Britons had reasons to resent the Romans, and the Iceni were joined by their neighbors, the Trinovantes. Boudicca led them through the chief Roman towns (modern Colchester, London, and St. Albans), slaughtering thousands. But when the main Roman army arrived, the Celts were defeated, and Boudicca killed herself.

Boudicca leads an attack on the Romans. It was unusual for a woman to lead an army, but women held high status among the Celts. Boudicca was not the only ruling queen in Celtic Britain.

Celtic leaders

In the long run, the Celts could not defeat the Romans. First, the trained, professional Roman army was superior to wild tribesmen, however brave. Second, the Celts were never united: one tribe might consider its neighbors a more dangerous enemy and therefore side with the Romans against them. In Gaul, Vercingetorix, king of the powerful Averni, came nearest to forming a Gallic coalition. He plotted rebellion against Julius Caesar, conqueror of Gaul, while Caesar was away in Britain in 54 B.C. A two-year campaign followed, fought with great brutality (the Romans killed captured civilians), until Vercingetorix was forced to retreat to his stronghold of Alesia. After a long, heroic defense, he had to surrender.

A gold coin of the Averni, a large tribe of southern Gaul, with the head of their great leader, Vercingetorix. Captured by the Romans at Alesia in 52 B.C., Vercingetorix was sent to Rome as a prisoner and executed eight years later.

Romanized Celts

The Gauls and Britons had established trade and other contacts with Rome 100 years or more before the conquest and were already partly "Romanized." Although they fought fiercely to keep their independence, the Celts soon came to accept Roman civilization. The Romans were sensible governors. They set up Roman administrations in the new provinces, and they imposed Roman law, but in general, they tried to adapt their government to the old arrangements. They did not force the Celts to give up all their own customs, and they left Celtic rulers in charge of their old lands. In fact, only 100 years after Caesar's conquest, Gauls sat in the Roman Senate and held high office in Rome. Roman rule brought many benefits, including (for many) a better standard of living, schools, written laws, and public services such as bathhouses and paved roads. Above all, it brought peace—the famous Pax Romana ("Roman peace").

This stone warrior of the first century B.C. comes from Gaul. He is a Celt (as seen by his torque), but the realistic style is Roman, and the Celts never carved free-standing figures like this until they experienced Mediterranean influence.

Local taxes were sometimes "farmed out" to men who paid a fee to be appointed tax collectors. This was a recipe for corruption and extortion, and many people complained. However, Roman officials themselves were also guilty.

Taxes

The benefits of Roman rule were many, but they were not cheap. Governments need money, which must come from taxes, and Rome expected its provinces to make a profit for the state. Under the emperors, each city or territory paid a regular tribute, based on an estimate of what it could afford. There were also indirect taxes, such as an inheritance tax and a tax on the sale of slaves. Roman officials in the provinces usually made a fortune at the taxpayers' expense.

This sculpture, The Dying Gaul, is a copy of one ordered by King Attalus I of Pergamum to commemorate his wars with the Celts in the second century B.C. Attalus was a sophisticated Greek ruler, but he respected the Celts, as this dignified sculpture shows.

Agriculture

The Celts had little to learn from the Romans in farming methods. Conditions in their cooler climate were different from the Mediterranean: some Mediterranean crops, notably olives, would not grow in the north. The Romans did introduce other crops, however, including various fruits and root vegetables.

Religion

The Romans, like the Celts, had a huge number of gods. Many of them can be traced to other peoples —the chief Roman gods were linked with earlier, Greek gods. In the same way, Roman and Celtic gods mixed and mingled. The Romans destroyed the druids because they feared their political influence, but otherwise they did not object to Celtic religion. They automatically associated Celtic gods with their own. To them, a Celtic blacksmith-god, for example, was simply a version of the Roman Vulcan.

This sculpture from Gaul in the first century A.D. shows how easily different religions mingled. The figure in the center is the Celtic god Cernunnos. On either side of him are the Roman gods Apollo and Mercury. Roman religious influence also encouraged the building of temples.

The most important new fruit in Gaul was the grape. The Gauls were already wine drinkers, but they brought grapes from the Mediterranean in boats up the Rhône. The great French wine-growing regions, such as Burgundy and Champagne, were first planted with vines in Roman times.

The Roman influence on architecture was strong, as the Celts did not build large public buildings, nor marble monuments such as this tomb of a rich Romano-Gallic family. Built about 10 years after Caesar's conquest, it shows that Roman influence was already well established.

Celtic rulers began minting their own coins in the third century B.C., probably inspired by Greek coins that they saw in the course of trade. Some show the ruler's head, and some have fine Celtic designs, such as this silver coin of the Norici (first century B.C.), from modern Hungary.

Clothes, jewels, cosmetics

Under Roman influence, well-to-do Celtic men and women adopted Roman dress and Roman style. Men put away their torques and shaved off their big moustaches. People dressed in the simple, loose-fitting costumes of the Mediterranean region, such as the Roman toga. They gave up wearing furs and trousers. In some ways the Romans followed the Celts. Roman women wore more gold jewelry after Rome gained control of Spanish gold mines. Most of the beauty aids known to women today were known to upper-class women of the first century A.D., who used all kinds of cosmetic instruments, including eyebrow pluckers and ear pickers.

Art and Architecture

The energetic, semi-abstract style of the La Tène culture was quite different from Classical Roman style. Whereas Roman artists tried to reproduce the real world, the Celts reproduced not its form but its spirit. But Roman design did not simply replace traditional Celtic designs. Rather, a combined style, called Romano-Gallic, developed. Although it represented reality, the Celtic spirit was also present, in flowing lines and restless movement.

Trade and Travel

The Celts had a well-developed network of trade routes throughout Europe and the Mediterranean. They exported slaves, furs, gold, iron, salt, and foodstuffs (salt-cured Celtic meats were considered a great delicacy in Rome). In return, they imported wine, Greek and Etruscan vases, ornate jewelry, and other luxury goods. Most of the goods traveled by river, mainly up the Rhône and the Saône. The city of Massalia (present day Marseille, in southeastern France), at the mouth of the Rhône, became an important market town. The Celts also traveled overland by foot, on horseback, and in two- or four-wheeled carts.

Cornish tin

Celtic Britain was largely self-sufficient and had only limited contact with continental Europe. The exception to this was Cornwall, with its rich tin mines. Tin was an essential component in making bronze, and traders from all over Europe flocked to the area from earliest times.

Ideas also flowed along the trade routes. The design of this Hallstatt jug, for example, shows how strongly Celtic potters were influenced by their Mediterranean counterparts.

A Celtic pick, used to extract salt.

Merchants were not the only people to be found along the wooded roads of ancient Europe. In this scene, the attention of the man with the yellow pants has been caught by something in the forest. According to legend, the druids celebrated important rites in the forests. This scene shows how the druids may have looked to traders passing by.

Salt

Salt was an important commodity for the Celts. Before refrigerators were invented, salting was the only way to preserve meat, fish, and many other products for any length of time. There were numerous salt mines in Gaul and throughout the Celtic world. Many of the salt-preserved Celtic products were exported.

The Celtic Fringes

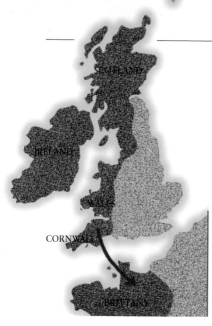

Dark areas show the Celtic-speaking regions

Ireland and the Scottish Highlands were never conquered by the Romans. Wales and Cornwall, in western Britain, also remained relatively untouched by the Roman occupation of England. As Roman power declined in the fourth and fifth centuries, Celtic peoples such as the Picts, from Scotland, and the Irish began to invade the Roman province. Then Germanic invaders from continental Europe, including the Angles and Saxons, started landing on the east coast of Britain. They clashed with the Celtic peoples and pushed them west again. Another important change at this time was the spread of Christianity, especially in Ireland, where it flourished. From Ireland, missionaries set out to Christianize much of Britain and Europe.

The Island Celts

The map shows those parts of the British Isles that remained largely Celtic. It also shows how the Bretons, the Celtic people of northeastern France, were pushed from Britain into France by the advance of the Irish from the west and the Germanic peoples from the east.

Prehistoric Celtic Ireland

Celtic Ireland before the fifth century A.D. was divided into four or five provinces, but each province had many small kingdoms that were often at war among themselves. Early Irish Celts traded with the Britons and Romans, and they adopted an art style that was their own version of the continental La Tène style.

Roman influence

Although they were never conquered by the Romans, Irish Celts traded with the Romanized Britons and were influenced by their culture.

This stone pillar is marked with the first Irish alphabet, known as Ogham, after the Irish god of eloquence, Oghma. The alphabet had 20 letters and is believed to have developed after Irish contact with Latin writing.

Torques are thought to have originated in Gaul. This gold torque was found in Ireland and is decorated in a local form of the La Tène style.

Picts and Scotti

During the fourth century, Irish pirates, or Scotti (a word that means "raiders"), began attacking Britain. They gradually established control over the Picts in northern Britain. The Scotti gave their name to this region, which is still known as Scotland.

Christianity in Ireland

According to legend, the Irish were converted to Christianity by St. Patrick's divine mission, beginning in the A.D. 440s. In reality, missionaries from Britain and Gaul probably began crossing to Ireland about A.D. 400. They entered a changing world that was very open to their message. Within 200 years, Christianity was well established. Monasteries became important centers, many wielding more power and influence than local rulers.

This silver and gold brooch was made in Scotland in about A.D. 700. It shows a combination of Pictish, Celtic, and Anglo-Saxon art styles.

St. Patrick (above) was born in Wales of Romanized Christian parents. He was kidnapped as a teenager and spent six years as a slave in Ireland before escaping to Gaul. He was ordained a priest and also became a bishop while in Gaul. From there, he moved to Ireland, where he began his famous mission. Today, St. Patrick is the patron saint of Ireland.

Elaborately carved Celtic crosses appeared in the 9th and 10th centuries. They were based on earlier wooden crosses used as grave markers.

The Golden Age of Ireland

The period from the seventh to ninth centuries is sometimes referred to as Ireland's "Golden Age." During that time, a remarkable civilization based on the Christian monasteries flourished and spread to other parts of the British Isles and also to Europe. The "Golden Age" ended with the Viking raids in the 9th and 10th centuries.

Irish monks produced beautiful, illuminated (illustrated) manuscripts. Their work combined traditional Celtic designs with Christian symbols and messages. This illustration is based on a drawing in The Book of Kells. *It shows Jesus being arrested.*

The "Tara" brooch, from County Meath. Tara was a famous seat of local kings.

The Irish monks were the first to write down Celtic myths and legends. Most of what is known of Celtic mythology dates from this time. The Ulster Cycle is one of the most famous groups of tales. This illustration (above) shows the young warrior Culann wrestling with a hound.

The scene below shows St. Columba, an Irish missionary, and his 12 disciples landing on the island of Ilona, on the west coast of Scotland. Columba, who was known as the Apostle of Caledonia (an ancient name for Scotland), converted the Picts to Christianity.

Irish missionaries

As Irish civilization bloomed, continental Europe was troubled by invasion, war, and poverty. Missionaries set off from Irish monasteries for Britain and mainland Europe. A second wave of Irish missionaries reached Europe during the ninth century, when they were driven out of the British Isles by the Viking raids. They brought a rich store of knowledge and ideas with them to Europe.

The Celts Live On

The Viking invasions of the 9th and 10th centuries, followed by the Norman Conquest in 1066, drove the Celts back to the western and northern parts of the British Isles—Ireland, Wales, Cornwall, and the Scottish Highlands—where they have remained to the present day. Fiercely independent and proud of their history and traditions, the Celts have clashed often with the English over the centuries. In recent years, Celtic languages and culture have been revived in an attempt to preserve them before they disappear entirely.

Robert the Bruce (1274–1329) seized the Scottish throne in 1306. He fought against England for most of his life to establish and maintain Scottish independence.

The Celtic inhabitants of Brittany, in France, also maintain their language and traditions. This woman is dressed in a tall lace cap to celebrate a Roman Catholic feast day.

This Welsh boy is learning Welsh Gaelic in school in modern Wales.

Ongoing Celtic and English rivalry

Over the centuries, the descendants of the Celtic and Anglo-Saxon peoples in the British Isles have mingled, but some forms of rivalry and conflict have also remained. The worst situation exists in Northern Ireland, where Protestant descendants of English settlers fight against Roman Catholic Irish inhabitants.

Traditions live on

Scottish Highlanders place great value on their traditions, which include the bagpipes, Highland dancing, tartans, kilts, haggis (a type of sausage), and traditional sports. Descendants of Highlanders who live in other parts of the world also value and preserve these traditions.

This young Scottish dancer leaps high above a pair of crossed swords during a competition at the Highland Games.

Celtic languages today

There are about two million people who can still speak one of the four surviving Celtic languages. The languages are Welsh, Breton, Irish Gaelic, and Scottish Gaelic. However, only about 500,000 people speak them on a daily basis, and the languages are in danger of dying out. To prevent this, attempts have been made to teach the languages in schools.

Celtic mysteries

The early Celts left no written records, and many mysteries about these ancient people remain. One mystery, the white horse carved into a hill at Uffington, in England, will probably never be solved. About 360 feet (110 m) long, the horse was made around 100 B.C., but is fully visible only from the air.

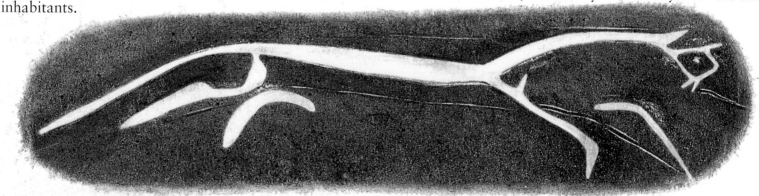

In this 14th-century illustration, dying King Arthur tells one of his knights to take his magic sword, Excalibur, back to the Lady of the Lake.

King Arthur

Legends about King Arthur, such as the drawing of Excalibur from a stone (right), date from the time of the Anglo-Saxon invasions of Britain, in the fifth to seventh centuries. Historians don't know whether Arthur existed, although it seems likely that the legends are based on the deeds of a brave warrior king. King Arthur was part of a warrior nobility that sat at the Round Table, and they are known as the Knights of the Round Table.

Sculpture of Irish immigrant Anie Moore, at Ellis Island, New York.

The new migrations

The Celts moved in huge numbers during the fifth and fourth centuries B.C. A second large-scale migration of their descendants took place in the 19th century, when famine, poverty, and eviction from the land forced millions of poor Irish and Scottish people to emigrate. Many went to the United States, but some also went to South America, Australia, and New Zealand.

Index

agriculture 39
alphabet 42
Alps 10, 11
Anatolia (see Turkey)
Anglo-Saxons 42, 44, 45
animals 11, 12, 14, 16, 18, 24, 25, 28, 30, 31, 32, 33, 35
architecture 39
aristocracy 9, 22
armor 21
art 8, 11, 28–29, 35, 39, 42
Asia 7
Australia 45
Austria 23, 28
– Hallstatt 8, 10, 26, 27, 41

Balkans 8, 10
banquets 34
barbarians 36
bards 14, 15, 22, 34, 35
bathhouses 38
Beltane 31
birds 18
blacksmiths 12, 25, 27
Bohemia 10
Book of Kells, The 43
Boudicca 23, 37
Bretons 42
Brigantia (see gods & goddesses, Brigid)
Britain 7, 8, 10, 11, 13, 24, 25, 33, 35, 37, 41, 42, 43, 44, 45
brochs 22, 26, 32
burial 9, 16–17

Caesar, Julius 11, 16, 31, 36, 37, 38, 39
calendars 30
– Coligny 31
Celtiberians 11, 18
cemeteries 16, 17
chariots 16, 20, 21, 26, 35
chiefdoms 8, 9
children 12, 22, 23, 35
clothing 11, 22, 23, 32, 39
coins 11, 28, 33, 39
cooking 16, 19, 25, 28
cosmetics 39
craftsmen 8, 12, 18, 22, 26, 28, 35
cremation 9, 17
crime 14
Cú Chulainn 15
Culann 43

diseases 16, 18, 31
druids and druidesses 12, 13, 14–15, 17, 22, 30, 31, 39, 41
– Dubthach 30
Dying Gaul, The 39

England 14, 17, 22, 26, 42, 44
– Bath 12
– Colchester 37
– Cornwall 41, 42, 44
– London 13, 37
– Maiden Castle 33
– Manchester 17
– Norfolk 26
– St. Albans 37

– Uffington 44
entertainment 30, 31, 34, 35
Etruscans 11, 36, 40
Europe 7, 10, 13, 17, 24, 25, 36, 40, 41, 42, 43
Excalibur 45

families 22, 24, 32
farming 8, 9, 18–19, 22, 23, 24, 25, 32, 39
feasts and festivals 16, 19, 30–31, 34, 35, 44
fish 18, 25
folk tales 7, 35
– Mabinogion, The 31
food 16, 18–19, 22, 24, 32, 34, 40
forts 9, 11
France 7, 16, 23, 42, 44
– Brittany 36, 44
– Burgundy 39
– Champagne 39
– Coligny 31
– Gascony 39
– Marseille 28, 40
– Paris 14
– Provence (Gallia Transalpina) 36
– Pyrenees 11
– Vix 16
Franks 36
funerals 16

gambling 35
games 30, 34–35
Gaul 7, 11, 13, 14, 16, 20, 31, 34, 36, 37, 39, 41, 42
Germany 17, 28
glassmakers 26, 28
gods & goddesses 12, 13, 14, 15, 17, 22, 27, 28, 30, 31, 35, 39, 42
– Apollo 39
– blacksmith-god 39
– Brigid 30
– Cernunnos 12, 13, 17, 39
– Dagda 13
– Dis Pater 30
– Earth Mother 12
– Epona 12, 28, 35
– Flidais 12
– Lugh 31
– Mabon 31
– Mercury 39
– Minerva 30
– Oghma 42
– Sulis 12
– Vulcan 39
goldsmiths 26
graves 7, 9, 16, 26
Greece 7, 10, 11, 28

Halloween 30
health 23
Highland Games 44
hill-forts 8, 9, 32, 33
houses & homes 23, 24–25, 33
Hungary 39
hunting 18, 25, 34, 35

Imbolc 30
Ireland 7, 10, 11, 13, 30, 35, 36,

42, 43, 44
– Kildare 30
– Northern Ireland 44
Italy 7, 10, 11, 36
– Apulia 36
– Bari 36
– Po valley 36

Jesus 43
jewelry 16, 26, 28, 29, 39, 40, 42, 43
– Tara brooch 43
– torques 42
judges 14

kings 37, 39, 45
– Arthur 45
– Attalus I 39
– Iceni 37
– Robert the Bruce 44
– Vercingetorix 36, 37

La Tène culture 8, 10, 11, 28, 29, 39, 42
legends 18, 35, 41, 43
– Ulster Cycle 43
Lindow Man 17
Livy (Roman historian) 36
Lughnasa 31

Massalia (see France, Marseille)
Mediterranean 8, 9, 11, 28, 32, 34, 36, 38, 39, 40, 41
merchants 41
Middle Ages 35
mining 8, 9, 26, 41
missionaries 42, 43
monasteries 42, 43
monks 7, 15, 35, 43
musical instruments 35

New Year 30
New Zealand 45
Norman Conquest 44

oppida 32, 33
ornaments 26, 28
Otherworld 12, 15, 28, 30, 35

peasants 34
pets 18, 24
Picts 42, 43
pirates 42
politics 15
Portugal 7, 11
pottery 19, 29
priests & priestesses 14, 15, 18

religion 12–13, 15, 39
– Christianity 30, 35, 36, 42, 43
– Protestantism 44
– Roman Catholicism 44
rivers 11, 39, 40
– Loire 15
– Rhine 11
– Rhône 39, 40
– Saône 40
– Seine 13
roads 38
Roman Empire 20, 36, 37

Romania 26
Romanization 11, 38–39
Romans 11, 12, 14, 17, 21, 28, 36–37, 38, 39, 42
Rome 7, 10, 11, 20, 28, 36, 37, 38
Round Table 45

sacrifices 12, 14, 16, 17, 31
saints 42, 43
– St. Columba 43
– St. Patrick 42
Samhain 30, 31
sanctuaries 12, 15
schools 38
Scotland 7, 10, 26, 32, 36, 42, 43, 44
– Hebrides 18
– Ilona 43
Scotti 42
sea 10, 11, 36
– Adriatic 36
– Black 10, 11
servants 24
shops 33
shrines 12, 13
Siculus, Diodorus (Greek historian) 22
slavery 9, 22, 38, 40
society 22–23
soldiers 11, 20, 22, 23
South America 45
Spain 7, 8, 10, 11, 20, 29
– Numantia 29
sports 18, 30, 34, 35
Switzerland 36

taxes 14, 38
technology 8, 26
temples 12, 13, 15, 33, 39
tools 16, 25, 28
towns 18, 32–33, 36
toys 35
trade 9, 11, 33, 36, 38, 39, 40–41
transport & travel 18, 40–41
tribes 7, 14, 22, 34
Turkey (Anatolia) 7, 10, 11
– Bosphorus 10
– Galatia 10
Tylis 11

Ukraine 7, 10
Underworld (see Otherworld)
United States of America 45
– New York 45

Vikings 43, 44
villages 8, 18, 29, 32–33

Wales 26, 36, 42, 44
war 9, 14, 15, 18, 20–21, 33, 35, 39, 42, 43
warriors 12, 13, 18, 20, 21, 22, 26, 30, 34, 35, 36, 38, 43
weapons 9, 11, 13, 16, 20, 28
weaving 23, 25
witches 15
– Nine Witches of Gloucester 15
women 15, 22, 23, 25, 37, 39
writing 22